This is Beth and this is Jill.
Jill is Beth's doll.

This is Puff. Puff is Beth's cat.
When Beth is in bed,
Puff gets Jill.

Puff is patting Jill.
He pats her into the bin!

The bin men have come to get the rubbish.

The men tip the bins into
the back of a big van.
Jill is in this bin bag!

Beth is sad.

She is missing Jill.

The bin men tip the rubbish into a big pit.

Lots of things are in the pit.
Pots, tubs, boxes . . . and Jill!

This is Tess. Tess is at the rubbish tip with her mum.

"Mum!" says Tess. "Is that a doll in the pit?"

A man picks up the doll.
He gives her to Mum.

Tess is in school. "This doll fell in a pit," she says.

"That's Jill!" says Beth.

Tess gives Jill back to Beth.

Beth gives Tess a set of peg dolls.